DE SU MOTOR

CONTENIDO NETO 450 ml

Cristina Paoli

Mexican Blackletter

Mark Batty Publisher | LLC

Dedicated to my Father, Mother & Jaime.

**Many Thanks to Paul McNeil from the
London College of Communication.**

Mexican Blackletter by Cristina Paoli.

Design: Cristina Paoli.

Production Manager: Christopher D Salyers.
Editing: Buzz Poole.

This book is typeset in: Univers Condensed, Univers Condensed
Oblique and Univers Condensed Bold.

Library of Congress Control Number: 2006932300

Printed and bound in China through Asia Pacific Offset.
Printed on 140 gsm Thai Woodfree.

10 9 8 7 6 5 4 3 2 1 First Edition

This edition © 2006
Mark Batty Publisher
36 W 37th Street, Penthouse
New York, NY 10018

www.markbattypublisher.com

ISBN-10: 0-9772827-8-3
ISBN-13: 978-09772827-8-4

Contents

4   **Introduction**
Why are Mexicans fond of Blackletter?

6   **Where it All Began**
8   Birth of Blackletter
9   Kinds of Blackletter

12   **How Blackletter Speaks**
14   Connotations of the Letterform
18   Approaching the Structure of Blackletter

20   **Mexican Blackletter**
22   Arrival into the New World
23   Why is Blackletter popular in Mexico

28   **Looking at Mexican Blackletter**
30   Categorization
54   Deconstruction of the Lettering
64   Just the Letter*form*
78   X-Rays

92   **Final Thoughts**

94   **Bibliography**

95   **Acknowledgments**

Introduction

Why are Mexicans fond of Blackletter?

Today in Mexico blackletter can be found mostly in folk functional graphics such as fascia lettering, signage, do-it-yourself advertisements and labels; it has also proven its popularity in tattoos, concert posters and less —but still present— in graffiti. Don't be mistaken by the contents of this book and believe that most folk Mexican lettering is set in blackletter, however. Unquestionably, most folk graphics use roman type in its serif or sans serif versions.

The purpose of this book is to show the presence and anatomy of blackletter in contemporary Mexico, and no examples of roman type are included. The blackletter that adorns countless small stores, shops and service providers all over Mexico has a long history that today enjoys a wholly Mexican twist that caters to the everyday needs of people, from plumbers to cobblers and everything in between. More than a way to create signage, Mexican blackletter speaks volumes about contemporary Mexican culture.

There are many explanations for why blackletter is popular in Mexico. The country's overwhelming colonial Spanish background is still present today, not only in the collective unconscious, but also in buildings, plazas and entire cities, some of which use blackletter in their signage to appeal to tourists, who visit these places to see colonial remnants.

Blackletter in Mexico is also associated with Christianity, from divine elegance to exuberant transcendence. Rooted in European religious traditions, the lettering possesses the quality of being above and beyond the normal. The same as the religious applications of blackletter instilled European practitioners with the importance of meditative devotion, the secular uses of blackletter in Mexico today convey the importance of such daily and simple practices as selling *tortas* or shoes, and symbolizes the fact that these acts are not just silly little hobbies, but people's lives. Why wouldn't a merchant or craftsperson advertise their service through a form that imparts a sense of lasting for a long time, or even being eternal?

Mexicans are fond of ornaments, color and contrast because they elicit laughter and fantasies, rituals and sense of place. One needs only to visit the nearest marketplace where all of this is bundled into one tangle of sensory overload. The songs of local music mix with the endless chatter of merchants hawking their wares, from an abundant range of fruits and vegetables, to herbs and plants sure to cure what ails you, to colorful textiles. Every step of the way, as often as the colors change, so too do the aromas wafting off piles and garlands of flowers, and the carts of food vendors, grilling, frying and peppering regional delicacies. This is a significant reality of everyday life in Mexico and the perfect point of entry for understanding the contexts in which blackletter is embraced and used.

The letterform's characteristics rely on ornaments and contrast, which are both playful and mysterious at the same time. The same as the market engulfs the shopper with its array of stimuli, the conjunction of blackletter characters overpowers the background. Blackletter heavily anchors the symbols by means of its robust structure. It is this structure of the blackletter shapes —amusing, flamboyant, even comical— that establishes the dialogue with the viewer.

Now you too have the chance to engage in this dialogue with the vast and varied hand-letterers working in and around Mexico City today. Read their signs, study the differences, appreciate the craftsmanship, and come to understand a very real facet of Mexico and Mexicans that transcends typography.

5

Where it All Began

Mexican
BlackLetter

Arrival in the New World

In 1492 Christopher Columbus arrived in America and by 1521, Hernan Cortés, on behalf of the Spanish crown, conquered Mexico, establishing the Colony of New Spain.

Jakob Kronberger (known as Jacobo Cromberger), the most important printer in Seville at the time, with the help of Juan de Zumárraga (first bishop of Mexico), established the first printing press on the American continent in Mexico in 1538.

Jacobo Comberger supplied all the materials and tools, such as press, movable types, ink and paper and sent one of his closest technicians, the Italian Giovanni Paoli (known as Juan Pablos) to be in charge of setting up and running the New World's first press.

In 1544, the fist printed book in America was published: *Doctrina Breve* by Fray Juan de Zumárraga, which was set in Rotunda blackletter, proving that movable types of blackletter were taken to Mexico and used on the printed matter of the time.

Later publications such as the example shown on the left, also used blackletter, although roman type was present too and widely used.

Below: Creamery and dried hot peppers 'Leo Day.' Grocery store and poultry shop 'Leo Dany.' Notice the difference in names; my guess is that the letterer missed the *n* on the left hand sign but decided to leave it as it is anyway.

Page 24: Airbrush illustration on Pick-up truck. 'Nacho' is a nickname for Ignacio. **Page 25 clockwise from top left:** Hairdresser. Jewelry shop. Hamburger street food stall. 'Jordana' cosmetics. Locksmith sign. Stationer sign.

Why is blackletter popular in Mexico?

From talking to the people that decorate their body with it, or that draw the letterform on a sign, I have discovered that Mexicans feel that blackletter communicates "tradition," or that "normal letters" –Roman type– just wouldn't be good enough for the particular message they need to express. More so, many who elect to employ blackletter for tattoos, signs and anything else imaginable believe that it takes the written message to a "religious" level and therefore, implicitly, associates the message with a kind of transcendence. In speaking with people, words such as "tradition," "religion," and "historical" continually surfaced.

For graffiti artists, the use of blackletter is a direct link to the "Cholo" (Mexican-American) culture, given that Cholos and Chicanos frequently select this letterform for tattoos, tags and murals. Many tend to describe it as "elegant" and others simply state that they use it because they "like it," and that's it, no need for more explanation. More times than not, in light of my questions, many people looked surprised and simply stated, "it's beautiful," "it's different" and for them that is all that matters. Just raising the question of why they choose blackletter made some people uncomfortable under the pressure of having to verbalize an un-rationalized aesthetic whim.

Blackletter results in a convenient medium of expression for many Mexicans when they want to associate their messages with a sort of transcendence, elegance, exuberance and sophistication, by means of which they are able to fulfill and transmit a hint of the cultural complexity mirrored in the robust, highly decorated letterform with its contrasting vertical and horizontal strokes. They choose a letterform that is charged with historical connotations that span the social, cultural and religious spectrums that have been simultaneously embraced, reinterpreted, modified, ignored and exposed in a game of double meaning, as we say in Mexico, of *albur*. An *albur* is a witty game of words between two or more subjects where double meanings are used with the intention of creating non-explicit or non-literal allusions to something else. The *albur* is commonly used as a foil for sexual connotations, but not exclusively.

By stating that blackletter is used in Mexico as an *albur* I mean that the people who select this letterform for such mundane purposes as the sign on a street food stall or to adorn the back of a pick-up truck with a name in blackletter and two beautiful woman in bikini swimsuits, are deliberately using the letterform to allude to the above mentioned connotations: elegance, tradition, religion, transcendence, etc. Knowing in advance that the medium and message have none of that, blackletter is nevertheless implemented to ventilate these meanings and laugh at the lack of them, establishing a dialogue full of humor and wittiness, to be enjoyed by the people who own the sign, and those that read it.

The choice of drawing a sign in blackletter is unto itself an open declaration of how the sign communicates the investment of time and money and how such an investment visually achieves more than any similar sign drawn with roman characters, especially in Mexico. When used, blackletter enhances written messages, converting them into elegant and transcendental discourses, regardless of the environment in which the sign is placed. In markets and food stalls or on streets, walls, trucks, and taxis. Regardless if it is drawn on cloth, an old metal plate or a piece of cardboard, blackletter has the ability to make known that which cannot be easily verbalized: history and how history manifests in the present.

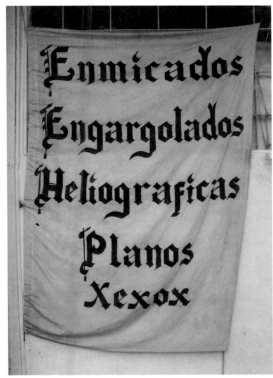

Below: Butcher and bacon shop.
Opposite page clockwise from top left: Cobbler street stall. Passenger bus. Suit store. Graffiti in a small Mexican town.

Blackletter in Mexico serves as a vehicle to express eccentricity and irreverent elegance; eccentric in the sense of being out of the center, beyond the center, moving towards something else, filled with energy and excitement, though it is not something unified in it's meaning. Irreverent elegance, because although the letterform is graceful and stylish, in Mexico it is used in the context of ordinary everyday life, dressing up signs of street *tacos*, cobblers or buses, that in reality lack a traditional sense of sophistication. Blackletter creates a new dynamic to the written words: the message expresses something that is beyond the taxi, the market, the wall on which it is drawn. We can consider blackletter as a message in itself, and as a pattern by which we can orient our psyche beyond explicit messages.

The popularity of blackletter in Mexico is related to the inherent qualities of Mexican culture: diversity and contrast. Mexico is a complex cultural spectrum marked by the collisions between the Spanish and the indigenous, but also African and Chinese influences among others. The diversity of religious beliefs, cultural traditions and geographic landscapes radiate through the many faces of Mexico and Mexicans, integrating through the recognition of this diversity while also contrasting in a new manner, inventive and creative.

Blackletter draws attention to its heaviness, formality, history and tradition. At the same time, however, in the context of Mexico, it evokes a transcendental playfulness, something that is out of the ordinary although it is tethered to daily life. Because Mexicans live in a country that thrives off such disparate contrasts, it is no wonder why blackletter, of all possible letterforms, is regularly selected to convey all of these dynamics through a few carefully executed brushstrokes.

looking
at Mexican
BlackLetter

Mexican blackletter can be analyzed on many levels from different points of view. It is as complex, playful and irreverent as Mexicans. One can rejoice in the microcosm of the single sign, enjoying the composition, choice of colors, spacing between characters and words, the implementation of the sign in the environment, or the erratic alteration of the letter shapes. One can take such analysis even further and speculate about the possible situations and personages that produced such eccentric typographical compositions.

Conversely, another approach is to isolate the characters, remove them from the context that produced them and concentrate solely on the anatomy of each letterform. Discover the variations of the shapes that can be found for a single letter of the alphabet. The viewer will discover that no character is identical to another, regardless if it belongs to the same sign, even if it is two of the same letters. Such detailed examinations permit viewers to appreciate the complexity and beauty of every stroke and ornament on every character.

Categorization

The majority of the photographs shown in this book are from the streets of Mexico City and some from smaller towns around the country.

The photographs are arranged in five different categories, responding to different variations in the lettering: Standard, Drop Shadow, Extended & Condensed, Extra Ornamental & Hybrids and Deviations & Unpredictable. The purpose is to familiarize the reader with the many forms that blackletter takes in the hands of Mexican hand-letterers and allow for an acquaintance of the context in which the letterform is used.

Condensed: These examples take the 'condensed' attribute of blackletter a little further, making extremely narrow characters, which in some cases highly compromise legibility.

1	2	3
4	5	6
7	8	9

1 Jewelry shop.
2 Shoe store.
3 Shoe store.
4 Metal pendants
5 Cobbler sign.
6 'Plumber and electrician.'
7 'Villa Rica' Venue.
8 Soft drink shop.
9 Notary.

Extra Ornamental & Hybrids

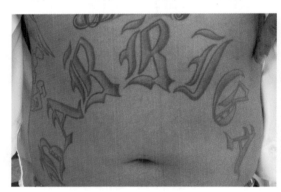

48

Extra Ornamental: Examples of extremely embellished letterforms where legibility is left aside in favor of the pure enjoyment of the form.

1	2	3
4	5	6
7	8	9
10	11	12

1 Jewelry shop.
2 Diamond shop.
3 Jewelry shop.
4 Lettering on bus.
5 Moving company truck.
6 6 Restaurants parking lot sign.
7 'Delicious hot tortas.'
8 Printing press sign.
9 Lettering on t-shirt.
10 Tattoo 'Barriga' last name, but also means tummy.
11 Tattoo 'Hinojosa' last name.
12 Tattoo 'Pacheco' last name, but also means stoned.

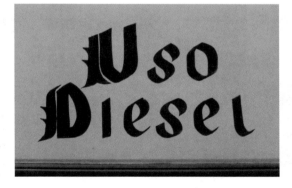

Hybrids: In these examples the blackletter style is recognizable. Nevertheless, they incorporate (or leave behind) some key characteristics, resulting in fascinating crossbreed characters.

1	2	3
4	5	6
7	8	9
10	11	12

1 'Hot tortas.'
2 'Delicious hamburgers and hot-dogs.'
3 'Hamburgers, French fries...'
4 Tizapan market.
5 Restaurant menu sign.
6 'Delicious tacos.'
7 Printing press sign.
8 'Professional tattoos and piercing.'
9 Boutique sign.
10 Bike repair service sign.
11 Lettering on bus. 'I use diesel.'
12 Lettering on bus 'Moon.'

MUDANZAS Y
FLETES. seru. LOCAL Y FORANEO
. TODA MANIOBRA

Jiménez C.
TEL. 56-19-51-06

CHEVROLET   CHEVROLET

y Compostura
de Todo Tipo
de Chapas y

Deviations & Unpredictable

52

Deviations: In some cases the unskilled hand of the letterer or the surface and materials available to work with, have a great influence on the letterform, resulting in deviations.

1	2	3
4	5	6
7	8	9
10	11	12

1 Stationer.
2 Stationer.
3 Toilet.
4 Moving company truck.
5 'Plumber and electrician.'
6 'Plumber and electrician.'
7 Watch repair service.
8 Watch repair service.
9 'Do not lay on the wall.'
10 'Genesis' 'and God said...'
11 'Welcome. Buenos Aires Hotel.'
12 Cantina (bar).

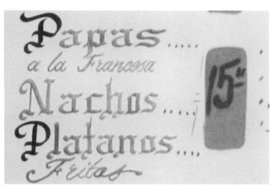

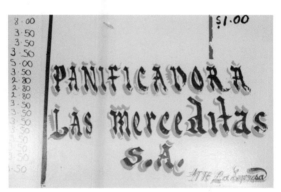

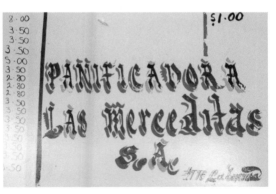

Unpredictable: A beautiful characteristic of Mexican hand lettering is its unpredictability. The examples above illustrate this feature.

1	2	3
1	2	3
4	5	3
4	5	

1 'Fixing of all kinds of locks and safety boxes.' Notice how the shape of the letter *C* changes thru the sign.

2 'Delicious sheep head.' On this sign, also the shape of the letter *C* varies, incorporating a swash stroke the second time it appears.

3 Menu sign in canteen. Observe how the swash on the letter *P* changes directions, and how it disappears on the second *E*.

4 Bakery. Notice how the shape of the letter *A* varies according to the space available.

5 Printing press 'The pet.' Observe how the last letter *a* is backwards. This is probably due to the fact that the letters are not drawn, but plastic cutouts pasted on the surface of the sign. It is likely that the last *a* was pasted backwards by mistake, and never fixed.

53

Left: Street food stall of *tortas* (Mexican sandwiches) outside a subway station in Mexico City. On the right hand side of the image are the cutout characters from the sign.

Deconstruction of the Lettering

After indulging in the context in which Mexican blackletter is used, and after placing it under the looking glass of categorization it becomes necessary –in order to fully appreciate the letterforms– to look at each character individually. The eloquent, playful and interesting shapes that constitute each and every character are revealed, exposed for the viewer to discover and take pleasure in. This idea led to the deconstruction of each one of the signs and letterings photographed, into single squares containing one letter and its background, which resulted in a collection of more than 1,400 individual characters (Uppercase, lowercase and numbers) that comprise this Mexican blackletter mosaic.

Letters are ambivalent signs: as images and abstractions, they are the signature of both intuition and mind.

Yvonne Schwemer-Scheddin

77

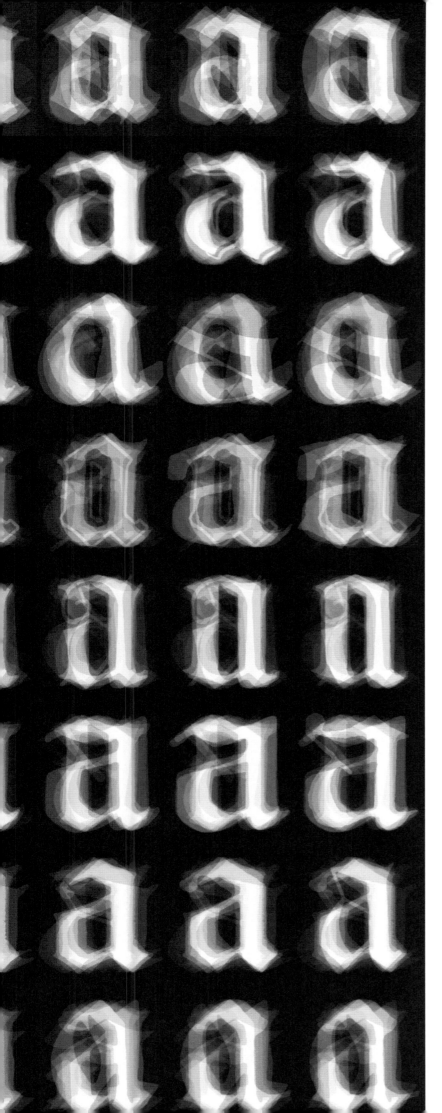

79

Left: This image represents the process of layering each one of the 87 *a* characters collected, to achieve a single image, the shape of which summarizes all of them.

X-Rays

The X-Rays are visual experiments created out of all the characters in *Just the letterform*. These were made by layering each one of the characters in order to achieve a single image, the shape of which summarizes all of them. The result is an X-Ray look-alike image of each letter of the alphabet (Upper and lowercase) and Numbers. In the cases of some letters, more than 80 characters are placed on top of one another, and in others it is a single layer. This is the result of the frequency of use for each letter in the Spanish language, although since the characters were taken from signage, labels and tattoos by no means is representative of the rate of recurrence of letters in Spanish written texts. For example the X-Ray of the lowercase *a* is composed by 87 characters, wile the letter *w* is only made out of 2.

80

Top and right: Complete set of uppercase, lower-case and numbers. The characters were made by layering each one of the collected characters in order to achieve a single image, the shape of which summarizes all of them.

ABCDEFGHIJ
KLMNOPQRST
UVWXYZ

abcdefghijklmno
pqrstuvwxyz

1234567890

NO SON LAS MEJORES PERO SI LAS MAS RICAS

Final Thoughts

The fundamental purpose of functional graphics and signage is to attract the attention of potential consumers and clients and effectively communicate the specific service or product being advertised. The establishments photographed for this book chose blackletter as a way to attract and communicate something about themselves. By doing so they embrace the letterform's rich history, while at the same time augmenting it with contemporary tweaks. Most importantly, they create new meanings and new forms that add to the cities and towns of Mexico.

The written messages displayed on signage are presented to the public, and if they gain the attention of the prospective customer –since it will be competing with many others– and on the basis of having a satisfactory level of legibility, it might be decoded.

Blackletter is not a legible letterform to the untrained eye. For those not accustomed to reading it on a regular basis, its forms might appear confusing and harder to read than roman type. In Mexico, which is not a country where blackletter is taught in the context of reading and writing, the widespread use of the letterform suggests that ultimately the decision to use it is purely an aesthetic whim.

In the case of signage, the importance of the typeface or lettering is crucial. This is the reason why great care must be taken in the selection and display of type. According to Tschichold (1992:13) "good lettering requires three elements: (1) Good letters. A beautiful letter form must be selected which is appropriate to purpose it is to serve and to the lettering technique to be used. (2) Good design in all details. This calls for well balanced and sensitive letter spacing and word spacing which takes the letter spacing into account. (3) A good layout. An har-

monious and logical arrangement of lines is essential. None of these three demands can be neglected".

Mexican blackletter folk functional graphics are probably the antithesis of Tschichold's rules for good lettering. (1) In many cases the letters are poorly drawn, virtually unreadable and arbitrarily chosen. (2) In most cases the spacing is absolutely random, erratic, and determined by the size of the surface of the sign. (3) The arrangement of the lines has more to do with the available space, than with a logical and harmonious layout.

These factors make no difference, however, and they certainly do not detract from the beauty or relevance of the designs. They all fulfill the utilitarian purpose of communicating the advertised service or product while also satisfying an aesthetic need, which is so important that it can be prioritized over the written message itself. They achieve a classic design goal: harmony between form and function.

The anatomy of Mexican folk functional graphics is determined by a technical casualness embedded in Mexican culture; many of these signs are made by professional hand-letterers, but many others are made by the people advertising their services or products. The results are signs full of spontaneity and typographical audacity.

The skilled or unskilled hand of Mexican letterers is what gives to Mexican blackletter its uniqueness, and its beauty. The desire to embellish the written language, in an effort to enhance the message and the environment that contains it, is what constitutes the very purpose of its use and popularity in Mexico.

CERRAJERIA
El Maestrito
SERVICIO A DOMICILIO
ES AL   tel. 539-53-39.

AQUI

ER OUTLET
Autos
la León y

COPIAS FA
FORROS
PARA
LIBROS

Bibliography

Bain, Peter and Paul Shaw (ed). (1998) **Blackletter: Type and national identity.** Canada: The Cooper Union.

Baines, Phil and Andrew Haslam. (2002) **Type & Typography**. London: Laurence King Publishing Ltd.

Baines, Phil; Catherine Dixon. (2003) **Signs. Lettering in the enviroment**. London: Laurence King Publishing Ltd.

Cohen, Marcel and Jean Sainte. (1992). **La escritura y la psicología de los pueblos.** México: Editorial Siglo XXI.

Dürer, Albrecht. (1965) **Of the just shaping of letters**. USA: Dover Publications Inc.

Fella, Edward. (2000) **Letters on America**. New York: Princeton Architectural Press.

Fischer, Steven Roger. (2005) **A History of writing**. London: Reaktion Books Ltd.

Gerstner, Karl. (2003) **Compendio para alfabetos**. Barcelona: Gustavo Gili Editorial.

Gill, Eric. (1988) **An essay on typography**. London: Lund Humphires Publishers Limited.

Heller, Steven (ed). (2004) **The education of a Typographer**. Canada: Allworth Press.

Henestrosa, Crisóbal. (2005) **Espinosa. Rescate de una tipografía novohispana**. México: Editorial Designio.

Kane, John. (2000) **A type primer**. London: Laurence King Publishing Ltd.

Kapr, Albert. (1983) **The art of lettering**. Germany: KG Saur Muchen.

Kinross, Robin. (2004) **Modern typography. An essay in critical history**. London: Hyphen Press.

Lafaye, Jacques. (2004) **Albores de la imprenta. El libro en España y Portugal y sus posesiones de ultramar (siglos XV y XVI)**. México: Fondo de Cultura Económica.

Lewis, John. (1978) **Typography. Design and practice**. London: Barrie & Jenkins Ltd.

Lupton, Ellen. (2004) **Thinking with type**. New York: Princeton Architectural Press.

Mena, Juan Carlos. (2002) **Sensacional. Mexican street graphics**. New York: Princeton Architectural Press.

Paz, Octavio. (2004) **El laberinto de la soledad**. México: Fondo de Cultura Económica.

Stols, Alexandre A.M. (1964) **Antonio de Espinosa. El Segundo impresor mexicano**. México: UNAM.

Tilson, Jake. (2004) **3 Found fonts**. London: Atlas.

Tschichold, Jan. (1995) **The New Typography**. California: University of California Press.

Updike, Daniel B. (1962) **Printing types. Their history, forms and use. A study on survivals**. Cambridge Massachussets: Belknap Press.

Acknowledgments

The author sincerely thanks all the people that in one way or another were involved in the making of this book.

Paul McNeil, from the London College of Communication, for his valuable advice and guidance. **Buzz Poole**, my editor, for endless readings and revisions of the text. **Antonio Paoli**, for his generous and vital advice. **Julia Pozas**, for her unconditional support and friendship. **Eduardo Sánchez** and **Sofía Broid**, for being who you are and share with me your passion for life and design. **Rodrigo Reyes**, for being the best companion in the search for Mexican blackletter. **Jaime Pontones**, for your constant help and advice. **Typophile.com**, for being the forum that brings together all kinds of type aficionados. **Mark Batty**, for believing in this project.

All my teachers, friends, family and colleagues; for all the knowledge and support you've given me throughout the years.

Image Credits

Roberto Barriga 'El Chankla', for allowing photographing his tattoo. Tatto: Barriga (Pages: 4 & 48) and the photographic trip to Xochimilco. **Alfredo Jardines 'Karroña'**, for sharing his tattoo creations and pictures. Tattoos: Pacheco and Hinojosa (Page: 48). **The anonymous tattoo artist from Patzcuaro**, Tatto: Tarasco (Page: 37). **Benjamín Estrada**, Punk posters (Pages: 17 & 96). **Daniel Castillo**, Carton box of Ilegal Squad aerosol spray cans (Page: 37). **Jimena Oliver**, photographs of headings signs (Pages: 6, 12, 20, 28). **Sofía Broid**, for allowing photographing her T-Shirt: Sofia (Page: 48). **Ana San Vicente**, Bus with lettering: Luna (Page: 49). **Biblioteca Nacional, Fondo Reservado**, First page from Gradualae Dominicale. Secundum normam missalis noui: ex decreto Sancti Concilij Tridén, Mexico 1576 (Page 22). **KG Saur Muchen**, Images from: Kapr, Albert. *The art of lettering* (Pages: 9-11). **The British Library**, Page from Luttrell Psalter. England, 1325-1335 (Page: 8).

All my gratitude and admiration to all the anonymous hand-letterers in Mexico, for their beautiful creations, which are a constant source of pleasure and inspiration to my work.

Design, **text**, **visual experiments** and **photographs** (except the for the ones listed in *Image Credits*): Cristina Paoli. **Text editing:** Buzz Poole. **Production Management**: Christopher D Salyers.
Printing, reproduction and **binding**: Asia Pacific Offset, China, 2006. **Paper**: 140 gsm Thai Woodfree. **Body text** and **headings typeface**: Univers Condensed, Univers Condensed Oblique and Univers Condensed Bold (Adrian Frutiger 1957). **Book title 'Mexican' typeface**: Zapfino (Hermann Zapf 1998).

Cristina Paoli is a Mexican Graphic Designer currently working in Mexico City. She studied Graphic Design at the University Iberoamericana in Mexico City and graduated with honors in 2004. She briefly worked in the studio of Alliance Graphique Internationale member, Gabriela Rodríguez, before moving to London where she undertook the MA Typo/Graphic Studies at the London College of Communication and graduated in December 2005. She currently works in the growing Design Studio 'S' where she is an associate partner.